Tea Cozy & Place Mats

Instructions on page 2.

Warm Hospitality

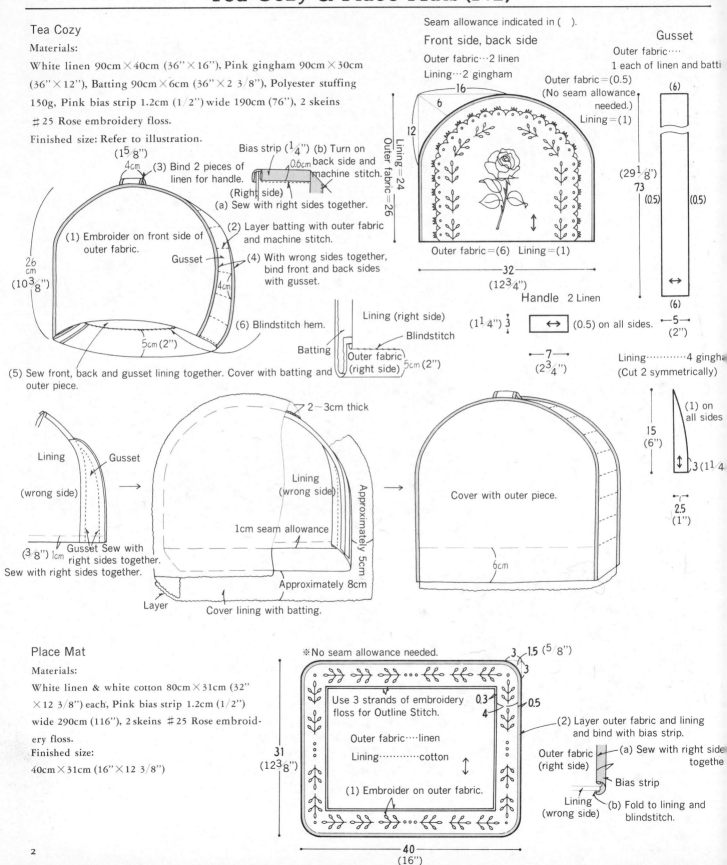

Tea Cozy

Materials:

White linen 90cm×40cm (36"×16"), Pink gingham 90cm×30cm (36"×12"), Batting 90cm×6cm (36"×2 3/8"), Polyester stuffing 150g, Pink bias strip 1.2cm (1/2") wide 190cm (76"), 2 skeins ♯25 Rose embroidery floss.

Finished size: Refer to illustration.

(1 5/8")
4cm
(3) Bind 2 pieces of linen for handle.

Bias strip (1/4") (b) Turn on back side and machine stitch.
0.6cm
(Right side)
(a) Sew with right sides together.

(1) Embroider on front side of outer fabric.

Gusset

(2) Layer batting with outer fabric and machine stitch.

(4) With wrong sides together, bind front and back sides with gusset.

26 cm (10 3/8")

4cm

(6) Blindstitch hem.

5cm (2")

(5) Sew front, back and gusset lining together. Cover with batting and outer piece.

Lining (right side)
Blindstitch
Batting
Outer fabric (right side)
5cm (2")

Seam allowance indicated in (   ).

Front side, back side
Outer fabric···2 linen
Lining···2 gingham

16
6
12
Lining = 24
Outer fabric = 26

Outer fabric = (6)   Lining = (1)

32 (12 3/4")

Gusset
Outer fabric····
1 each of linen and batti
Outer fabric = (0.5) (No seam allowance needed.)
Lining = (1)

(6)
(29 1/8")
73
(0.5)   (0.5)
(6)

Handle 2 Linen
(1 1/4") 3
↔ (0.5) on all sides.
7 (2 3/4")
5 (2")

Lining··········4 gingha
(Cut 2 symmetrically)

(1) on all sides
15 (6")
3 (1 1/4
2.5 (1")

Lining (wrong side)
Gusset
(wrong side)
Gusset Sew with right sides together.
(3/8") 1cm
Sew with right sides together.

2~3cm thick
Lining (wrong side)
1cm seam allowance
Approximately 5cm
Layer
Cover lining with batting.
Approximately 8cm

Cover with outer piece.
6cm

Place Mat

Materials:

White linen & white cotton 80cm×31cm (32" ×12 3/8") each, Pink bias strip 1.2cm (1/2") wide 290cm (116"), 2 skeins ♯25 Rose embroidery floss.

Finished size:
40cm×31cm (16"×12 3/8")

※No seam allowance needed.

3 1.5 (5/8")
3

Use 3 strands of embroidery floss for Outline Stitch.

Outer fabric····linen
Lining·········cotton

(1) Embroider on outer fabric.

31 (12 3/8")

0.3
0.5
4

(2) Layer outer fabric and lining and bind with bias strip.

Outer fabric (right side)
(a) Sew with right side togethe
Bias strip
Lining (wrong side)
(b) Fold to lining and blindstitch.

40 (16")

Actual size

2 in

1 out

Do Feather Stitch and finish as shown in diagram.

3 strands

3 strands Chain Stitch

2 strands Satin Stitch

center

3 strands Outline Stitch

Place Mat :
Position in designated place.

Finished line

Center

3

Tablecloth
Instructions on page 6.

Materials:

White linen 140cm×140cm (56"×56"),

Blue linen 140cm×20cm (56"×8"),

14 skeins ♯25 Blue embroidery floss.

Finished size:

138cm×138cm (55 1/4"×55 1/4") square.

Directions:

Embroider white linen. Sew border with blue linen.

Actual size c

Use 4 strands of embroidery floss
for Outline Stitch.

A

A'B'C' and ABC are embroidered symmetrically.

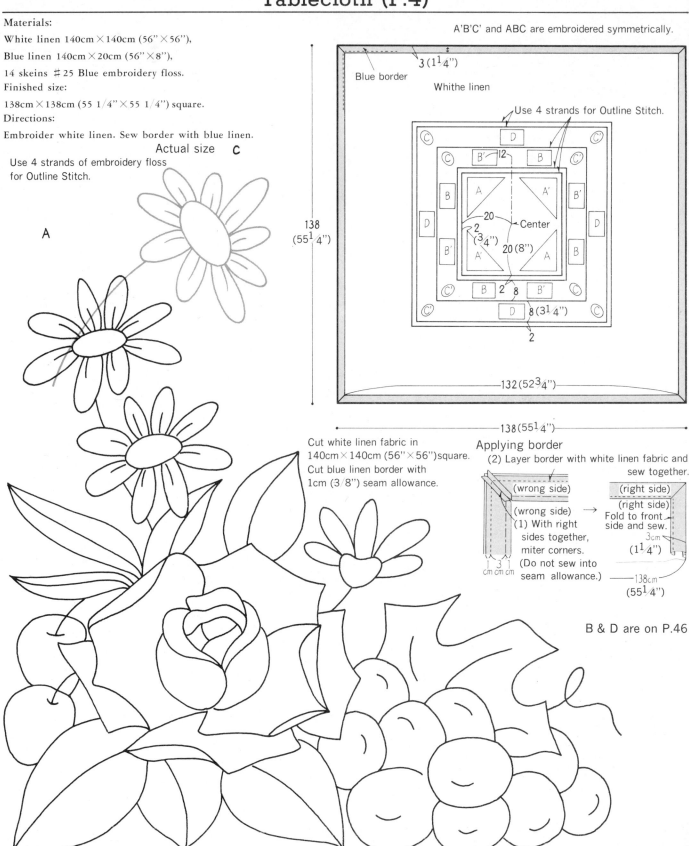

Blue border

Whithe linen

Use 4 strands for Outline Stitch.

D

C   B'   12   B   C'

B   A   A'   B'

20   Center

2
(3 4")

20(8")   A'   A   B

C   B   2   8   B'   C

D   8(3 1/4")

2

138
(55 1/4")

132 (52 3/4")

138(55 1/4")

Cut white linen fabric in
140cm×140cm (56"×56")square.
Cut blue linen border with
1cm (3/8") seam allowance.

Applying border

(2) Layer border with white linen fabric and
sew together.

(wrong side)

(wrong side)

(1) With right
sides together,
miter corners.
(Do not sew into
seam allowance.)

1 3 1
cm cm cm

(right side)

(right side)

Fold to front
side and sew.

3cm
(1 1/4")

138cm
(55 1/4")

B & D are on P.46

Use #25 embroidery floss.
Do Outline Stitch using
3 strands unless
indicated otherwise.

Lazy Daisy Stitch
Use 3 strands.

Chain S
Use 2
strands.

Satin S
Use 2
strands.

Chain Stitch
Use 2 strands.

French Knots
(one twist
French Knots)
Use 4
strands.

Satin Stitch
Use 3
strands.

Feather S
Use 2 strands.

Chain Stitch
Use 3 strands.

Outline S
Use 2
strands.

Chain S
Use 3
strands.

Twisted
Chain S
Use 2
strands.

Satin Stitch
Use 2 strands.

Napkins,
Napkin Rings
& Coasters
Instructions on page 10.

8

Napkins

Materials:

Blue-gray linen 38cm×38cm (15 1/4"×15 1/4") square

(for 1), ♯25 embroidery floss in gray-brown, gray,

blue, white and blue-gray for hemming (1 skein each).

Finished size:

35cm×35cm (14"×14") square

Use Outline Stitch unless indicated otherwise.

Actual size

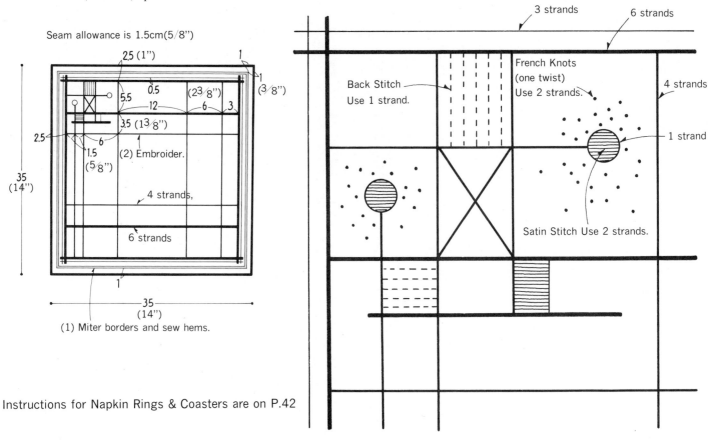

Seam allowance is 1.5cm(5/8")

2.5 (1")
1
0.5
5.5
(2 3/8")
12
6
3
3.5 (1 3/8")
2.5
6
1.5 (5/8")
(2) Embroider.
4 strands,
6 strands
35 (14")
1

35 (14")

(1) Miter borders and sew hems.

3 strands — 6 strands

Back Stitch Use 1 strand.

French Knots (one twist) Use 2 strands.

4 strands

1 strand

Satin Stitch Use 2 strands.

Instructions for Napkin Rings & Coasters are on P.42

Mitering Corners and Finishing Hems

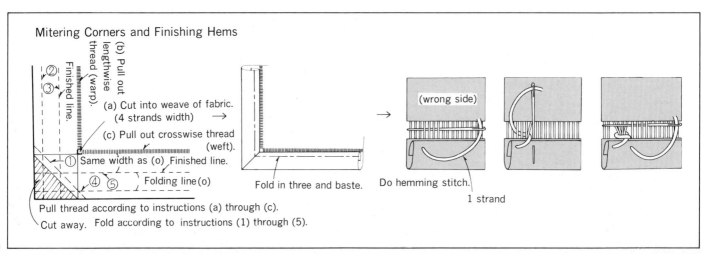

(b) Pull out lengthwise thread (warp).

Finished line.

Finished line.

② ③

(a) Cut into weave of fabric. (4 strands width)

(c) Pull out crosswise thread (weft).

① Same width as (o) Finished line.

④ ⑤ Folding line(o)

Pull thread according to instructions (a) through (c).

Cut away. Fold according to instructions (1) through (5).

Fold in three and baste.

(wrong side)

Do hemming stitch.

1 strand

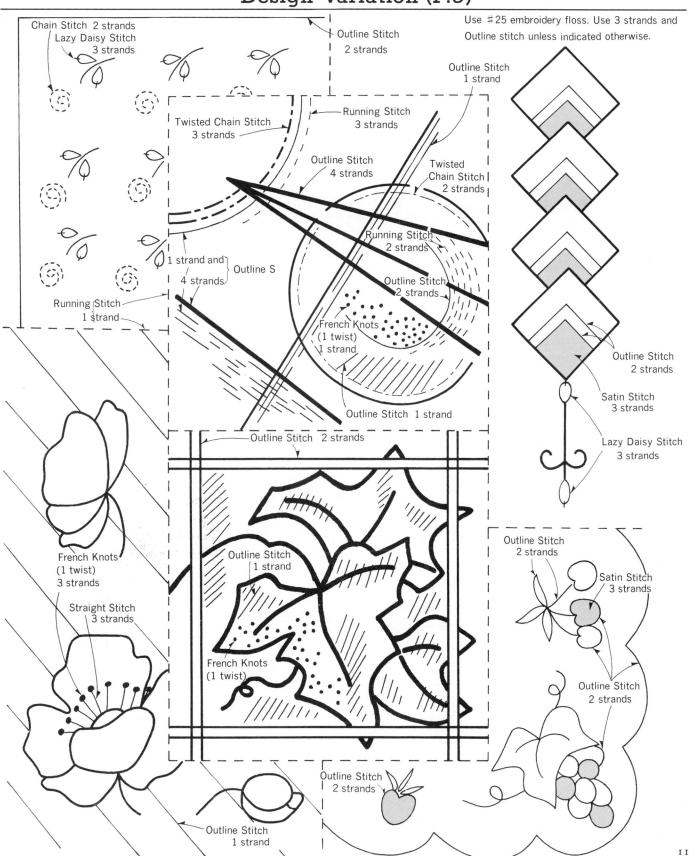

Chain Stitch 2 strands
Lazy Daisy Stitch
3 strands

Outline Stitch
2 strands

Use #25 embroidery floss. Use 3 strands and
Outline stitch unless indicated otherwise.

Outline Stitch
1 strand

Twisted Chain Stitch
3 strands

Running Stitch
3 strands

Outline Stitch
4 strands

Twisted
Chain Stitch
2 strands

Running Stitch
2 strands

Outline Stitch
2 strands

1 strand and
4 strands

Outline S

French Knots
(1 twist)
1 strand

Running Stitch
1 strand

Outline Stitch 1 strand

Outline Stitch
2 strands

Satin Stitch
3 strands

Lazy Daisy Stitch
3 strands

Outline Stitch 2 strands

Outline Stitch
1 strand

Outline Stitch
2 strands

Satin Stitch
3 strands

French Knots
(1 twist)

French Knots
(1 twist)
3 strands

Straight Stitch
3 strands

Outline Stitch
2 strands

Outline Stitch
2 strands

Outline Stitch
1 strand

11

KITCHEN

Shelf Lining

Instructions on page 14.

Embroidery
Shelf Lining (PP.12, 13)

Materials:

(for 1)

Blue & white gingham 57cm × 68cm (22 3/4" × 27 1/4"), 1 skein Ultramarine blue #25 embroidery floss.

Finished size:

55cm × 32cm (22" × 12 3/4")

(2) With right sides together, sew front and back sides leaving opening.

notch

1cm (3/8")

Trim seam allowance.

Seam allowance is 1cm (3/8").

(4") opening

(3) Turn inside out and fold seam allowance inside. Machine stitch edge.

1 each of front and back side

(1) Embroider design on right side.

KITCHEN   KITCHEN

2.5 (1")

11 (4 3/8")

55 (22")

32

Use 3 strands and Satin Stitch unless indicated otherwise.

Actual size

Back Stitch 3 strands

Back Stitch 3 strands

KITCHEN

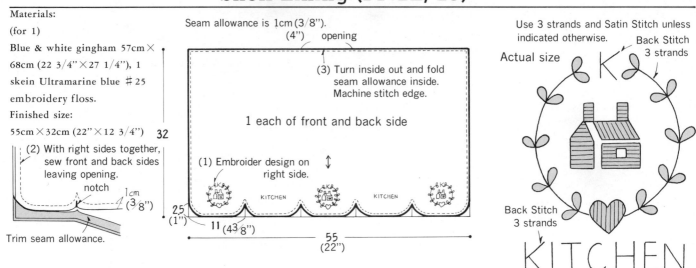

Continued from P.26

Round Shape

Materials:

16cm × 16cm (6 3/8" × 6 3/8") square each of : green cotton
        white cotton
        flannel
        batting,

No seam allowance needed.

Outer section······1 each of white cotton, flannel and batting

Back section······1 green cotton

10cm (4")   (1/4")   0.8cm

Fold bias strip in half and blindstitch.

Back section
Blindstitch (right side)

(3) Make handle and attach to back.

16 (6 3/8")

0.8 (1/4")

CLUB KITCHEN CLUB

Running S 3 strands

(1) Embroider outer piece.

(2) Layer outer piece, flannel, batting and backing. Bind with bias strip.

bias strip

0.8 cm (1/4")

(b) Fold to back and blindstitch.

Backing (wrong side)

Outer piece (right side)

(a) Sew with right sides together.

Green bias strip 1.6cm (5/8") wide 62cm (24 3/4"), Moss-green #25 embroidery floss.

Finished size :

16cm (6 3/8") diameter

Use 2 strands and Back Stitch unless indicated otherwise.

Actual size

Running Stitch 3 strands

Back Stitch 3 strands

CLUB
KITCHEN
CLUB

Square Shape

Materials:

17cm (6 3/4"×6 3/4") square each of : beige
cotton flannel batting,
Brown & white gingham 20cm×20cm (8"×8")square,
Dark brown cotton 16cm×3cm (6 3/8"×1 1/4"),
1 skein Dark brown #25 embroidery floss.

Finished size :

17cm×17cm (6 3/4"×6 3/4") square

No seam allowance needed.

Outer section······1 each of beige cotton 17cm×17cm (6 3/4"×6 3/4"),
flannel & batting

Backing··········· 1 Gingham 20cm×20cm (8"×8")

Handle············· Dark brown Cut 16cm×3cm

(3) Blindstitch.   (6 3/8"×1 1/4")

5cm (2")

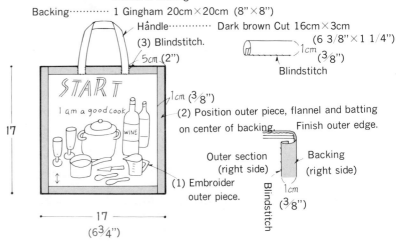

1cm (3/8")
Blindstitch

(2) Position outer piece, flannel and batting
on center of backing.   Finish outer edge.

Outer section
(right side)

Backing
(right side)

(1) Embroider
outer piece.

Blindstitch

1cm
(3/8")

17
(6 3/4")

Use 3 strands and Back Stitch unless indicated otherwise.

Actual size

Outline Stitch
3 strands

15

Miniature Cushions
Instructions on page 18.

Miniature Cushions (PP.16, 17)

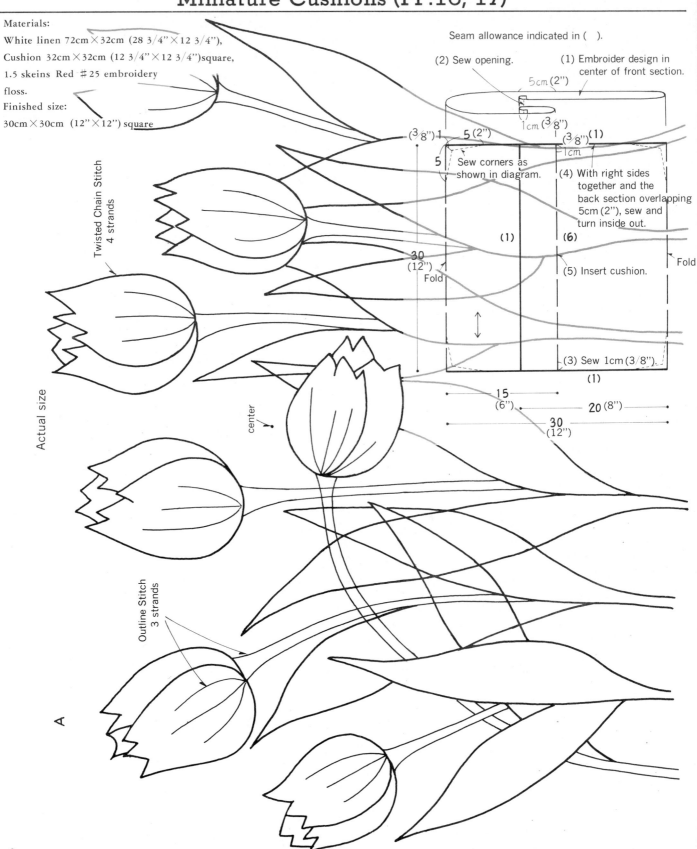

Materials:

White linen 72cm×32cm (28 3/4"×12 3/4"),

Cushion 32cm×32cm (12 3/4"×12 3/4")square,

1.5 skeins Red #25 embroidery

floss.

Finished size:

30cm×30cm (12"×12") square

Twisted Chain Stitch
4 strands

Actual size

center

Outline Stitch
3 strands

A

Seam allowance indicated in ( ).

(2) Sew opening.

(1) Embroider design in center of front section.

5cm (2")

1cm (3/8")

(3/8")1

5 (2")

(3/8")(1)

5

1cm

Sew corners as shown in diagram.

(4) With right sides together and the back section overlapping 5cm (2"), sew and turn inside out.

(1)

(6)

30 (12")

Fold

(5) Insert cushion.

Fold

(3) Sew 1cm (3/8").

(1)

15 (6")

20 (8")

30 (12")

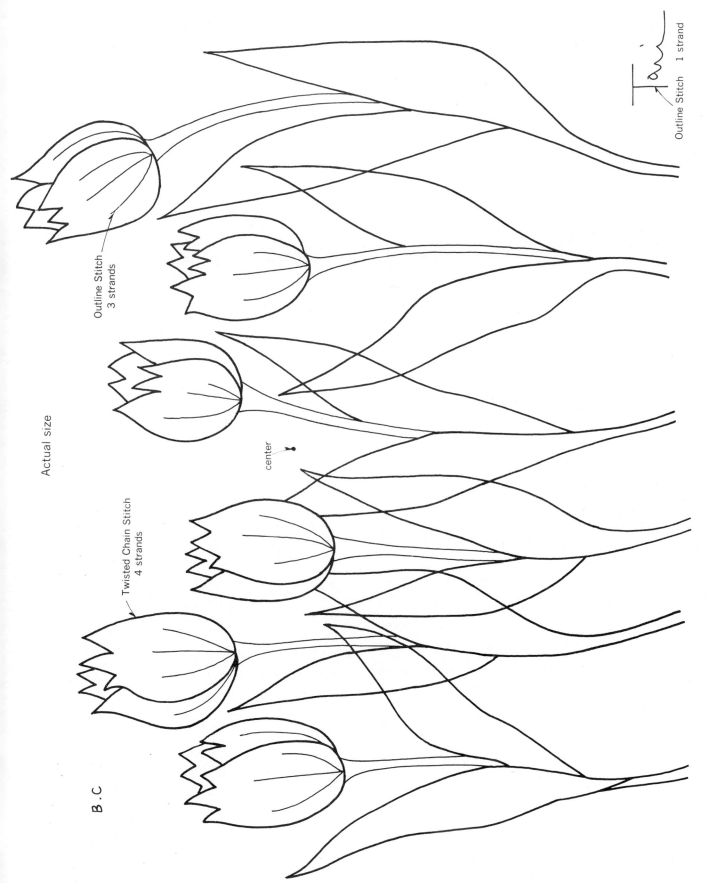

Actual size

Outline Stitch 1 strand

Outline Stitch 3 strands

Twisted Chain Stitch 4 strands

center

B.C

Housework Can Be Fun!

Pantry Cart Cover

Instructions on page 22.

Embroidery

Pantry Cart Cover (PP.20,21)

Materials:

Red Broadcloth 74cm×100cm (29 5/8"×40"), Patchwork fabric (refer to picture), 0.5 skein White #25 embroidery floss.

Finished size:

52cm×68cm (20 3/4"×27 1/4")

Patchwork fabric

(refer to picture)······52 pieces

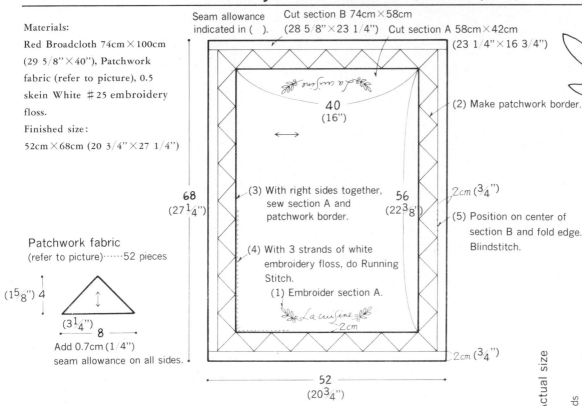

Seam allowance indicated in ( ).

Cut section B 74cm×58cm (28 5/8"×23 1/4") Cut section A 58cm×42cm (23 1/4"×16 3/4")

(15⁄8") 4

(31⁄4") 8

Add 0.7cm (1/4") seam allowance on all sides.

40 (16")

68 (27 1⁄4")

56 (22 3⁄8")

52 (20 3⁄4")

2cm (3⁄4")

2cm (3⁄4")

2cm

de La cuisine

La cuisine

(2) Make patchwork border.

(3) With right sides together, sew section A and patchwork border.

(4) With 3 strands of white embroidery floss, do Running Stitch.

(1) Embroider section A.

(5) Position on center of section B and fold edge. Blindstitch.

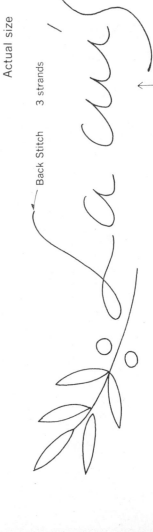

Actual size

Back Stitch   3 strands

Back Stitch

center

La cuisine

Continued from P.38

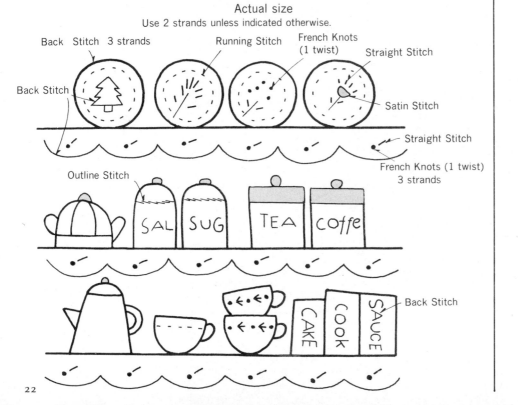

Actual size
Use 2 strands unless indicated otherwise.

Back   Stitch   3 strands

Running Stitch

French Knots (1 twist)

Straight Stitch

Back Stitch

Satin Stitch

Straight Stitch

French Knots (1 twist)
3 strands

Outline Stitch

SAL   SUG   TEA   COFFE

CAKE   COOK   SAUCE

Back Stitch

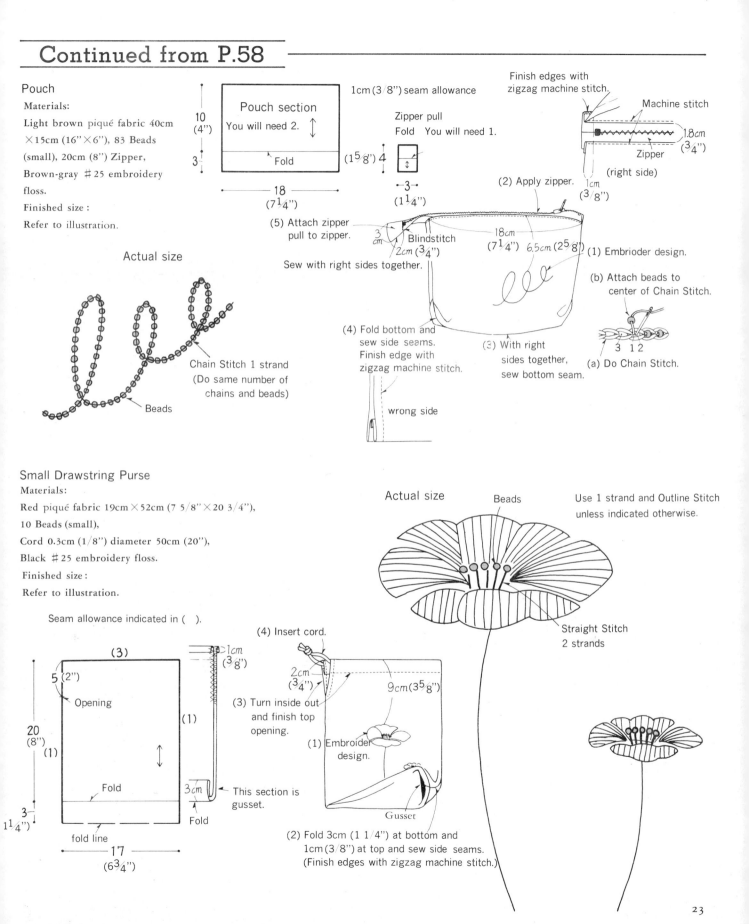

Pouch

Materials:

Light brown piqué fabric 40cm
×15cm (16"×6"), 83 Beads
(small), 20cm (8") Zipper,
Brown-gray #25 embroidery
floss.

Finished size :

Refer to illustration.

1cm (3/8") seam allowance

Pouch section
You will need 2. ↕

10 (4")

3

Fold

18
(7 1/4")

(1 5/8") 4

Zipper pull
Fold   You will need 1.

3
(1 1/4")

↕

Finish edges with
zigzag machine stitch.

Machine stitch

Zipper

(right side)

1.8cm
(3/4")

1cm
(3/8")

(2) Apply zipper.

Actual size

Chain Stitch 1 strand
(Do same number of
chains and beads)

Beads

(5) Attach zipper
pull to zipper.

Sew with right sides together.

3 cm

Blindstitch

2cm (3/4")

18cm
(7 1/4")   6.5cm (2 5/8")

(1) Embrioder design.

(b) Attach beads to
center of Chain Stitch.

3 1 2

(a) Do Chain Stitch.

(4) Fold bottom and
sew side seams.
Finish edge with
zigzag machine stitch.

(3) With right
sides together,
sew bottom seam.

wrong side

Small Drawstring Purse

Materials:

Red piqué fabric 19cm×52cm (7 5/8"×20 3/4"),

10 Beads (small),

Cord 0.3cm (1/8") diameter 50cm (20"),

Black #25 embroidery floss.

Finished size :

Refer to illustration.

Seam allowance indicated in ( ).

(3)

5 (2")

Opening

20
(8")

(1)

(1)

Fold

3

1 1/4")

fold line

17
(6 3/4")

1cm
(3/8")

(1)

3cm

Fold

This section is
gusset.

Actual size

Beads

Use 1 strand and Outline Stitch
unless indicated otherwise.

Straight Stitch
2 strands

(4) Insert cord.

(3) Turn inside out
and finish top
opening.

2cm
(3/4")

9cm(3 5/8")

(1) Embroider
design.

Gusset

(2) Fold 3cm (1 1/4") at bottom and
1cm (3/8") at top and sew side seams.
(Finish edges with zigzag machine stitch.)

Toaster Cover & Potholder

Toaster Cover
Instructions on page 27.
Potholder
Instructions on page 26.

24

SWEET CORN

FROM MY HEART

START

I am a good cook

WINE

Mitten

Materials:

Green shirting fabric 50cm×30cm (20"×12"), Green & white gingham 70cm×30cm (28"×12"), Batting 90cm ×30cm (36"×12"), Off-white #25 embroidery floss.

Finished size:

Refer to illustration.

Instructions for round and square potholders are on P.14.

(2) With right sides together, sew outer sections and batting. Turn inside out.

(3) With right sides together, sew lining and insert into outer section.

(1) Embroider design on outer section.

(b) Fold to back and blindstitch.

Outer section (right side)

(a) Sew with right sides together

Bias strip 2 cm (3/4")

(4) Bind opening with bias strip.

(5) Attach handle to lining and machine stitch.

Handle : Cut gingham. 14cm×4cm (5 5/8"×1 5/8")

26 cm (10 3/8")

(3/4")

6cm

(0.8)

Bias strip :

Cut bias strip from gingham. 32cm×6cm (12 3/4"×2 3/8")

Align fabric grain.

1cm (3/8")

Machine stitch

Actual size

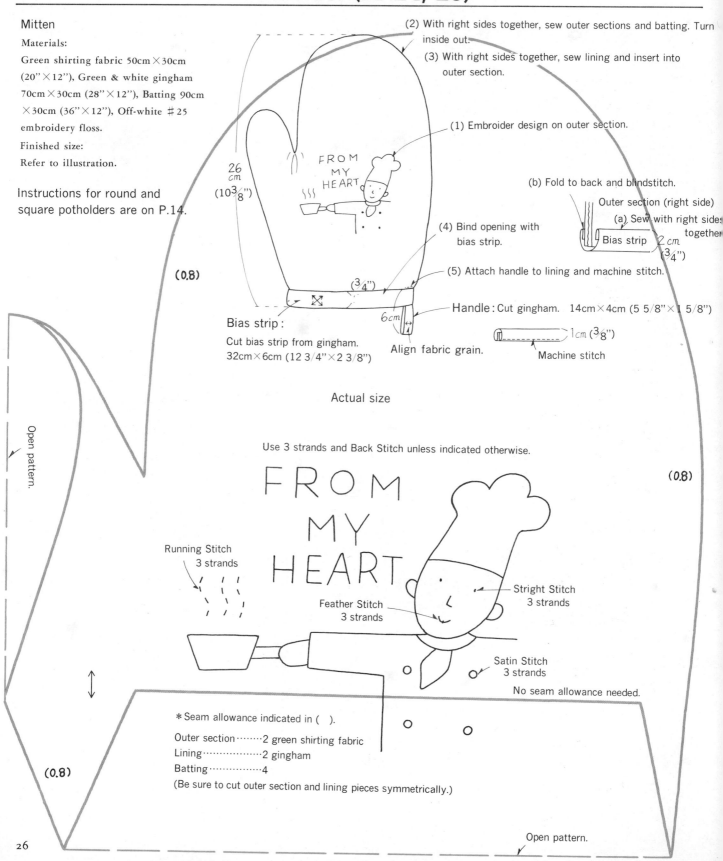

Use 3 strands and Back Stitch unless indicated otherwise.

FROM MY HEART

Running Stitch 3 strands

Feather Stitch 3 strands

Stright Stitch 3 strands

Satin Stitch 3 strands

No seam allowance needed.

Open pattern.

(0.8)

(0.8)

*Seam allowance indicated in ( ).

Outer section·······2 green shirting fabric
Lining················2 gingham
Batting···············4

(Be sure to cut outer section and lining pieces symmetrically.)

(0.8)

Open pattern.

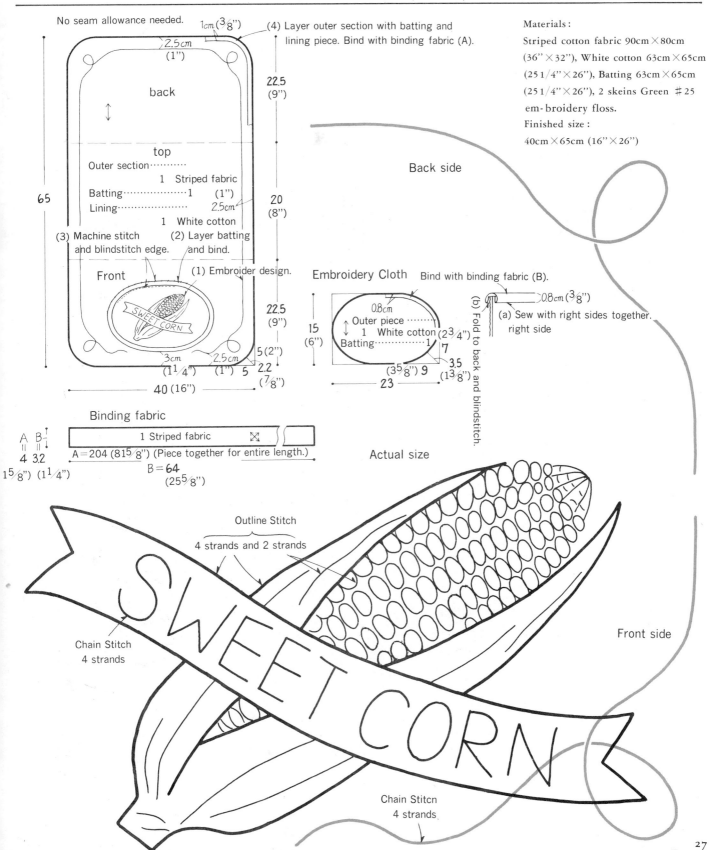

No seam allowance needed.

1cm (3/8")

2.5cm (1")

(4) Layer outer section with batting and lining piece. Bind with binding fabric (A).

back

top

Outer section··········
1 Striped fabric

Batting···········1 (1")

Lining ···········2.5cm
1 White cotton

(3) Machine stitch and blindstitch edge.

(2) Layer batting and bind.

Front

(1) Embroider design.

22.5 (9")

20 (8")

22.5 (9")

5 (2")
2.2 (7/8")
5

65

40 (16")

3cm (1 1/4")   2.5cm (1")

Materials :
Striped cotton fabric 90cm×80cm
(36"×32"), White cotton 63cm×65cm
(25 1/4"×26"), Batting 63cm×65cm
(25 1/4"×26"), 2 skeins Green #25
em- broidery floss.
Finished size :
40cm×65cm (16"×26")

Back side

Embroidery Cloth   Bind with binding fabric (B).

Outer piece ·········
1   White cotton
Batting·········1

0.8cm

0.8cm (3/8")

(b) Fold to back and blindstitch.

(a) Sew with right sides together. right side

15 (6")

(2 3/4")
7

(3 5/8") 9

3.5 (1 3/8")

23

Binding fabric

1 Striped fabric

A B
‖ ‖
4 3.2
1 5/8") (1 1/4")

A=204 (81 5/8") (Piece together for entire length.)

B=64 (25 5/8")

Actual size

Outline Stitch
4 strands and 2 strands

Chain Stitch
4 strands

Front side

Chain Stitch
4 strands

Rice Cooker Cover
& Kitchen Cloth

Rice Cooker Cover
Instructions on page 30.
Kitchen Cloth
Instructions on page 30.

Materials:

Soft pink linen 42cm×42cm (16 3/4"×16 3/4")
square, 1.5 skeins Brown #25 embroidery floss.

Finished size:

40cm×40cm (16"×16")

Seam allowance is 1cm (3/8").

Actual size

Do Outline Stitch unless indicated otherwise.

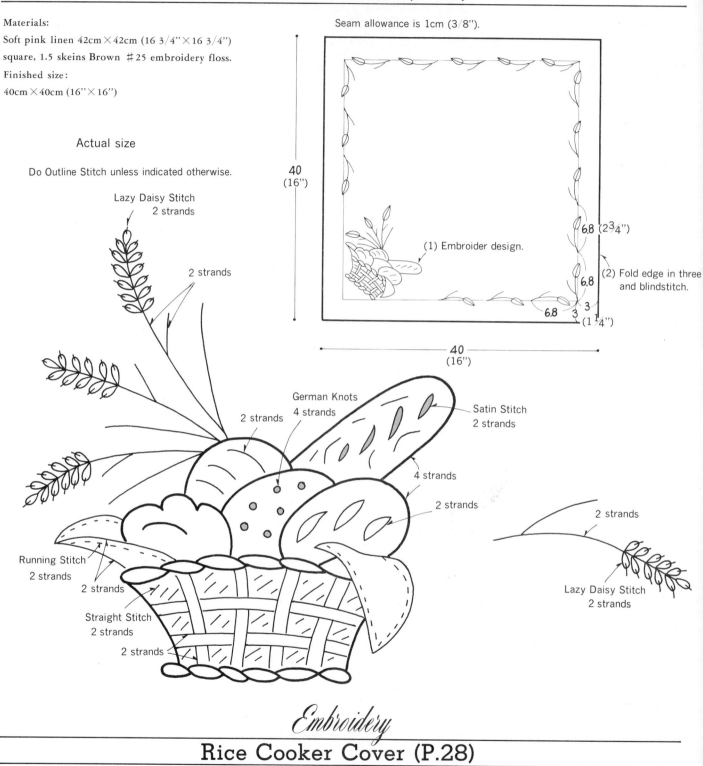

Lazy Daisy Stitch
2 strands

2 strands

German Knots
4 strands

Satin Stitch
2 strands

2 strands

4 strands

2 strands

2 strands

Running Stitch
2 strands

2 strands

Straight Stitch
2 strands

2 strands

Lazy Daisy Stitch
2 strands

40
(16")

6.8 (2³4")

6.8

(1) Embroider design.

(2) Fold edge in three
and blindstitch.

6.8

3 1
3 1
6.8 (1¼4")

40
(16")

Materials:

Embroidered cotton fabric 50cm×100cm (20"×40"),

White cotton (for lining) 60cm×100cm (24"×40"),

Patchwork fabric & appliqué fabric (refer to picture),

Batting   60cm×100cm (24"×40"),

Piping strip 1.5cm (5/8") wide 195cm (78"),

3 skeins Crimson #25 embroidery floss.

Finished size:

Refer to illustration.

Top section

15
(6")

15

Outer fabric ········· 1 — Embroidered cotton fabric
Lining ·················· 1 — White cotton
Batting ··············· 1

Cut lining and batting together.

Seam allowance indicated in ( ).
Add 1cm (3/8") seam allowance.

Handle

Embroidered cotton fabric
No seam allowance needed.

10
(4")

Add 1cm (3/8") seam allowance.

Side section

Outer fabric····Embroidered cotton fabric
Lining··········Cut 1 each of white cotton and batting 97×28cm (38 3/4"×11 1/4") (seam allowance included)

14
(5 5/8")

95 (38")

Patchwork fabric
(Refer to picture)······

38 pieces

Add 0.7cm (1/4") seam allowance.

2 3/8") 6

← 5 →
(2")

Appliqué fabric
(Refer to picture)········

8 pieces

Add 0.7cm (1/4") seam allowance.

5

← 5 →

Bias fabric   1 White cotton
No seam allowance needed.

2
(3/4")

97cm (38 3/4")

(piece together for entire length)

(10) Sew a running stitch around handle piece. Make a ball with batting and place on handle piece. Pull thread to make ball.

(8) With right sides together, sew top and side sectinos with piping strip inserted between. (Finish edge with zigzag machine stitch.)

(4) Layer outer fabric, batting and lining. With right sides together, sew side seam. (Finish edge with zigzag machinestitch.)

(5) Use 4 strands and Outline Stitch in-the-ditch, making sure you stitch only the outer fabric and batting.

(7) Layer outer fabric, batting and lining of top section. Appliqué pieces to layered top section.

(6) Sew with right sides together.

(3) Sew with right sides together.

(1) Embroider design 5 times on outer fabric.

(2) Make patchwork border.

26 cm
(10 3/8")

95cm

(9) Insert piping strip and finish edge.

Piping strip
Machine stitch
1cm (3/8")
1cm
0.5cm (1/4")
Side section | Bias fabric
(right side) | (wrong side)

↓

Side section (wrong side)
Blindstitch
1cm (3/8")
Bias fabric (right side)

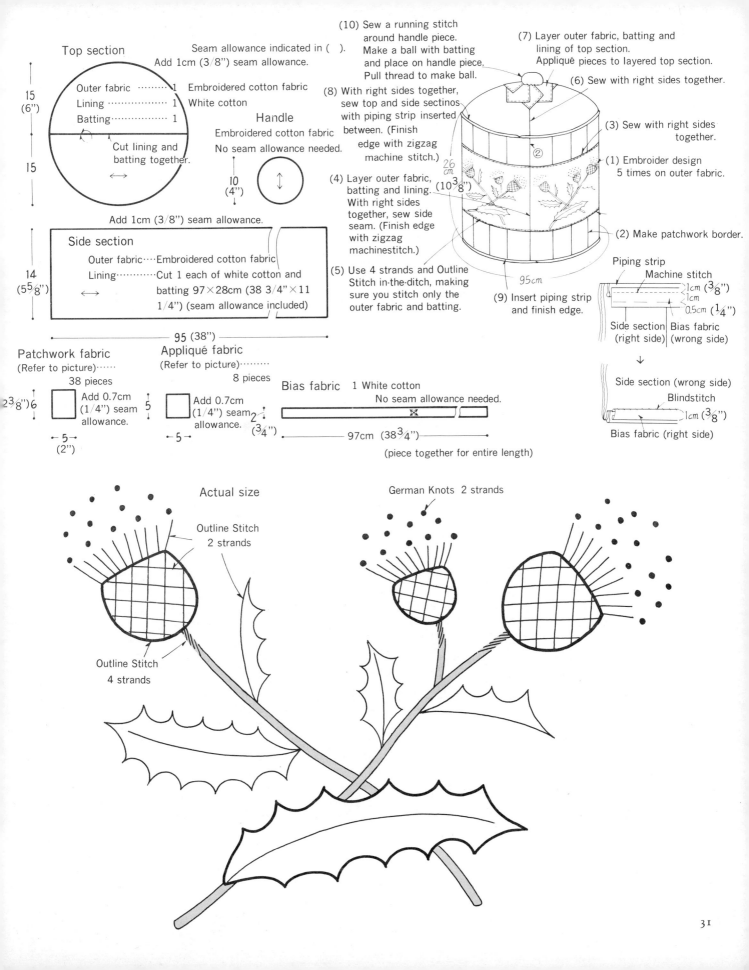

Actual size

German Knots 2 strands

Outline Stitch
2 strands

Outline Stitch
4 strands

Apron
Instructions on page 34.

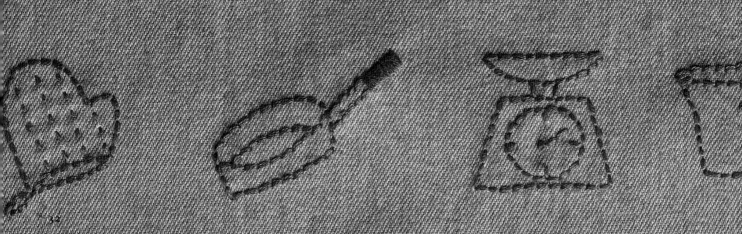

PUMPKIN

GARLIC

POTATO

TOMATO

THÉ   CAFÉ   SUCRÉ

COOKY

Materials:

Blue soft denim 135cm×110cm (54"×44"),

2 pairs Suspender fasteners,

1 pair Snaps,

0.5 skein Blue #25 embroidery floss.

Finished size:

Refer to illustration.

Actual size

Use 6 strands of embroidery floss.

― Running Stitch

― Back Stitch

Satin Stitch

French Knots (1 twist)

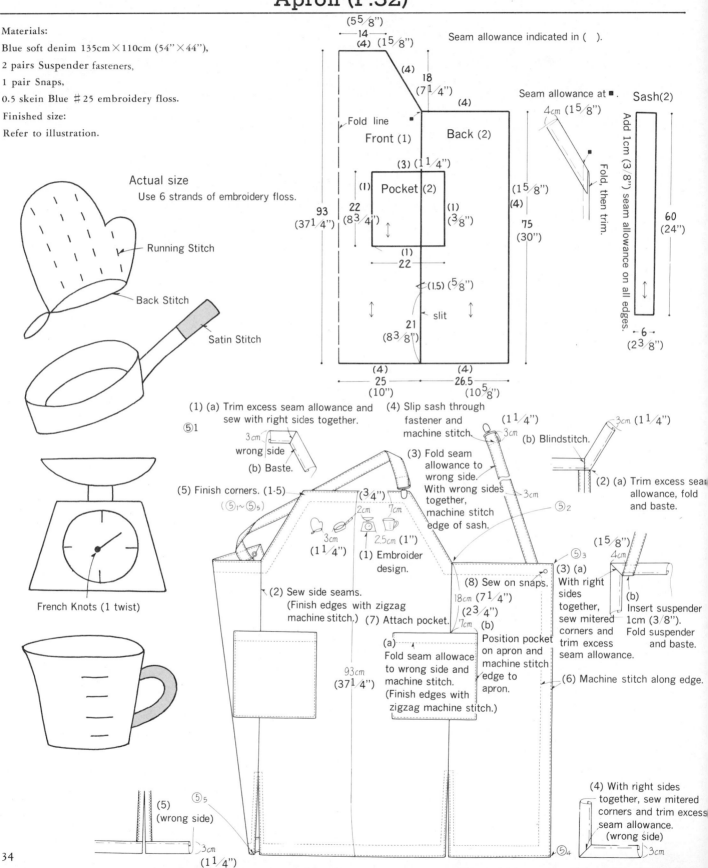

Seam allowance indicated in ( ).

Seam allowance at ■.   Sash(2)

Add 1cm (3/8") seam allowance on all edges.

(5 5/8")
14
(4) (1 5/8")
Fold line
Front (1)
18 (7 1/4")
(4)
Back (2)
4cm (1 5/8")
Fold, then trim.
(3) (1 1/4")
(1)   Pocket (2)   (1)
22 (8 3/4")   (1) (3/8")
93 (37 1/4")
(1 5/8")
(4)
75 (30")
60 (24")
(1)
22
(1.5) (5/8")
slit
21 (8 3/8")
6 (2 3/8")
(4)   (4)
25 (10")   26.5 (10 5/8")

(1) (a) Trim excess seam allowance and sew with right sides together.

⑤1

3cm wrong side

(b) Baste.

(4) Slip sash through fastener and machine stitch.

(3) Fold seam allowance to wrong side. With wrong sides together, machine stitch edge of sash.

3cm

3cm (1 1/4")
(b) Blindstitch.

⑤2

(2) (a) Trim excess seam allowance, fold and baste.

(5) Finish corners. (1-5)
(⑤1~⑤5)

(3 4")
2cm   7cm
3cm
(1 1/4")   2.5cm (1")

(1) Embroider design.

⑤3

(1 5/8")
4cm

(3) (a) With right sides together, sew mitered corners and trim excess seam allowance.

(b) Insert suspender 1cm (3/8"). Fold suspender and baste.

(8) Sew on snaps.

(2) Sew side seams. (Finish edges with zigzag machine stitch.)

18cm (7 1/4")
(2 3/4")
7cm

(a) Fold seam allowace to wrong side and machine stitch. (Finish edges with zigzag machine stitch.)

(7) Attach pocket.

(b) Position pocket on apron and machine stitch edge to apron.

93cm (37 1/4")

(6) Machine stitch along edge.

(5) (wrong side)
⑤5
3cm (1 1/4")

⑤4

(4) With right sides together, sew mitered corners and trim excess seam allowance. (wrong side)
3cm

Embroidery
Design Variation (Actual size) (P.33)

Use strands #25 embroidery floss
and Back Stitch unless indicated otherwise.

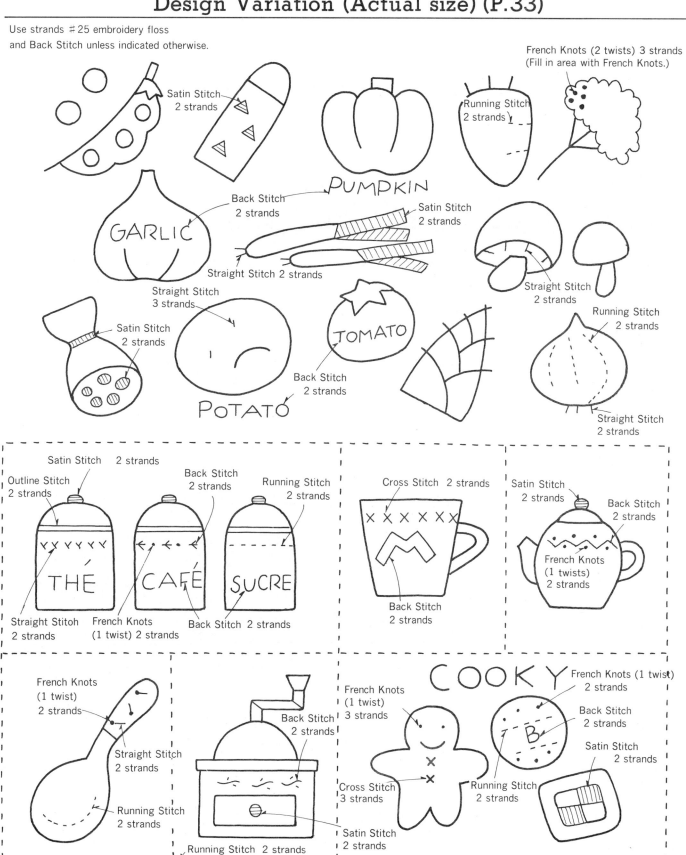

35

Apron
Instructions on page 38.

Materials:

Navy-blue shirting fabric 90cm×310cm (36"×124"),

Elastic 0.6cm (1/4") wide 20cm (8"),

1 White button 2cm (3/4") diameter,

0.5 skein Sand beige #25 embroidery floss.

Finished size:

Refer to illustration.

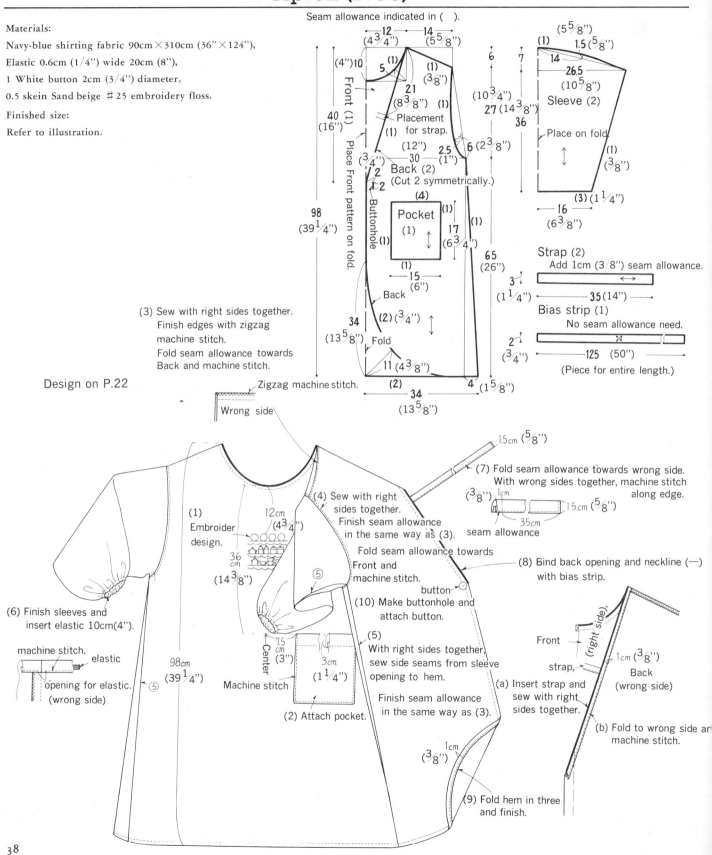

Seam allowance indicated in ( ).

Front (1)   Place Front pattern on fold.

12 (4¾") — 14 (5⅝")

(4")10   5 (1)   (1) (3⅜")

21 (8⅜") (1)

Placement for strap.

(1) (12")   30   2.5 (1")   6 (2⅜")

(¾")   2   2   Back (2) (Cut 2 symmetrically.)

40 (16")

98 (39¼")

Buttonhole

Pocket (4)
(1)   (1)
17 (6¾")   (1)
15 (6")
(1)

Back   (2) (¾")
34 (13⅝")   Fold

11 (4⅜")   (2)   34 (13⅝")   4 (1⅝")

Sleeve (2)   (5⅝")   1.5 (5⅝")
(1)   14
26.5 (10⅝")
Place on fold
6   7
(10¾")   27 (14⅜")   36
(1) (3⅜")
(3) (1¼")
16 (6⅜")

65 (26")

Strap (2)   Add 1cm (3/8") seam allowance.
3 (1¼")   35 (14")

Bias strip (1)   No seam allowance need.
2 (¾")   125 (50")   (Piece for entire length.)

(3) Sew with right sides together. Finish edges with zigzag machine stitch. Fold seam allowance towards Back and machine stitch.

Design on P.22

Zigzag machine stitch.   Wrong side

(1) Embroider design.

12cm (4¾")

36 cm (14⅜")

(4) Sew with right sides together. Finish seam allowance in the same way as (3).
Fold seam allowance towards Front and machine stitch.

(7) Fold seam allowance towards wrong side. With wrong sides together, machine stitch along edge.
1.5cm (5⅝")
(3⅜") 1cm   1.5cm (5⅝")
35cm
seam allowance

(8) Bind back opening and neckline (—) with bias strip.

button

(10) Make buttonhole and attach button.

(6) Finish sleeves and insert elastic 10cm (4").

machine stitch.   elastic
opening for elastic. (wrong side)

98cm (39¼")

⑤

Center
7.5 cm (3")

3cm (1¼")

Machine stitch

(2) Attach pocket.

(5) With right sides together, sew side seams from sleeve opening to hem. Finish seam allowance in the same way as (3).

Front   (right side)
strap,   1cm (3⅜")
Back (wrong side)
(a) Insert strap and sew with right sides together.
(b) Fold to wrong side and machine stitch.

(9) Fold hem in three and finish.
(3⅜") 1cm

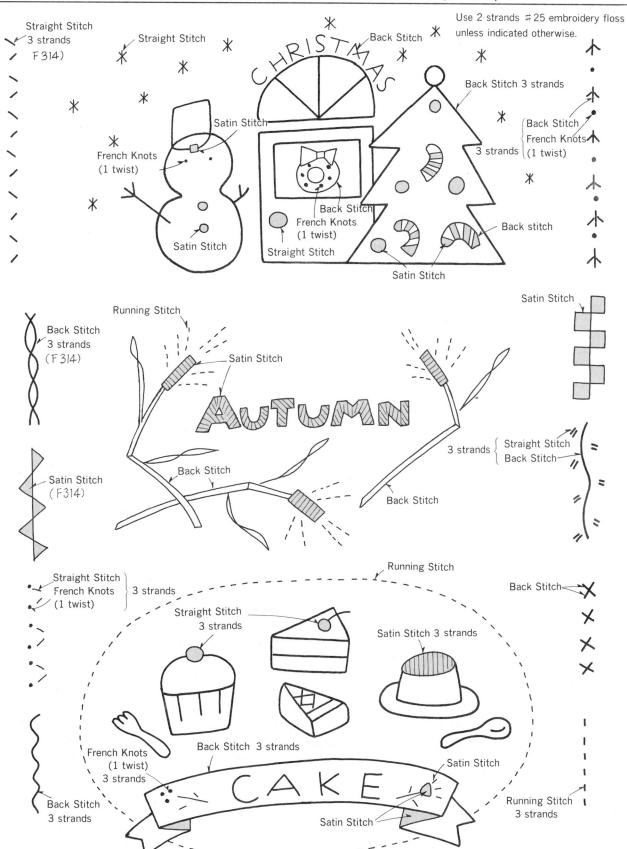

Use 2 strands #25 embroidery floss unless indicated otherwise.

Straight Stitch 3 strands (F 314)

Straight Stitch

Back Stitch

Back Stitch 3 strands

Back Stitch French Knots (1 twist) 3 strands

Satin Stitch

French Knots (1 twist)

Back Stitch French Knots (1 twist) Straight Stitch

Satin Stitch

Back stitch

Satin Stitch

Back Stitch 3 strands (F 314)

Running Stitch

Satin Stitch

Satin Stitch

Satin Stitch (F314)

Back Stitch

3 strands Straight Stitch Back Stitch

Back Stitch

Running Stitch

Straight Stitch French Knots (1 twist) 3 strands

Straight Stitch 3 strands

Satin Stitch 3 strands

Back Stitch

French Knots (1 twist) 3 strands

Back Stitch 3 strands

Satin Stitch

Back Stitch 3 strands

Satin Stitch

Running Stitch 3 strands

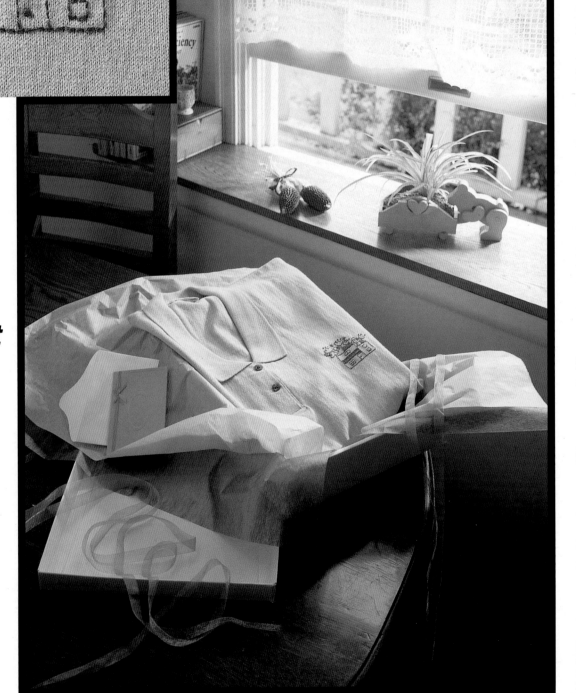

Creative Embellishments

Polo Shirt

Instructions on page 42.

ICE CREAM

BIG PRESENT

GOOD MORNING

CANDY TREE

Embroidery
Polo Shirt (P.40)

Materials:

Short sleeve polo shirt,

Blue-purple ♯25 embroidery floss.

Directions:

Embroider design on left side of shirt.

Use 3 strands unless indicated otherwise.

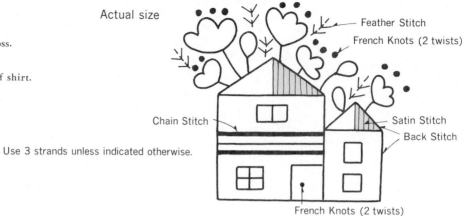

Actual size

Feather Stitch

French Knots (2 twists)

Chain Stitch

Satin Stitch

Back Stitch

French Knots (2 twists)

Continued from P.10

Napkin Ring

Materials:

Gray & light brown linen 30cm×8cm
(12"×3 1/4") each, Bias strip 1.2cm
(1/2") wide 120cm (48"), 8 pairs

Snaps (small), Blue, gray, gray-brown,
white ♯25 embroidery floss.

Finished size:

15cm×4cm (6"×1 5/8")

No seam allowance needed.

Outer fabric ······4 gray

Lining ··············4 light brown

(1⁵⁄₈")4

15
(6")

Actual size

Do Outline Stitch unless indicated otherwise.

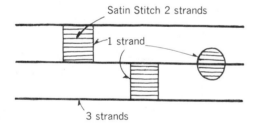

Satin Stitch 2 strands

1 strand

3 strands

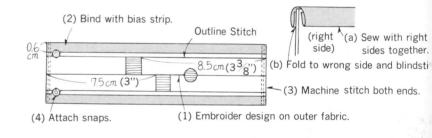

(2) Bind with bias strip.

Outline Stitch

0.6 cm

8.5cm(3³⁄₈")

7.5cm (3")

(4) Attach snaps.

(1) Embroider design on outer fabric.

(right side)

(a) Sew with right sides together.

(b) Fold to wrong side and blindsti

(3) Machine stitch both ends.

Coaster

Materials:

Beige & light brown linen 20cm×10cm
(8"×4") each, Blue-gray linen 20cm×
20cm (8"×8") square, Brown bias
strip 1.2cm (1/2") wide 180cm (72"),

Blue, gray, gray-brown, white ♯25
embroidery floss.

Finished size:

10cm×10cm (4"×4") square.

No seam allowance needed.

Outer fabric ······2 each of beige,
light brown

Lining ··············4 blue-gray

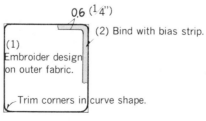

0.6 (¹⁄₄")

(2) Bind with bias strip.

(1) Embroider design on outer fabric.

10

Trim corners in curve shape.

10

Actual size

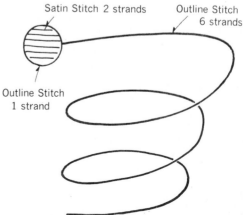

Satin Stitch 2 strands

Outline Stitch
6 strands

Outline Stitch
1 strand

Design Variation (Actual size) (P.41)

Use 3 strands #25 embroidery floss
unless indicated otherwise.

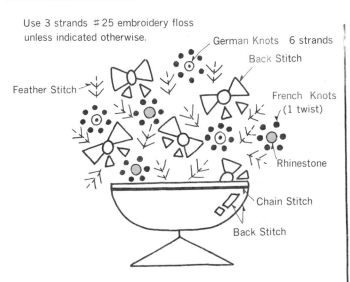

Feather Stitch

German Knots   6 strands

Back Stitch

French Knots
(1 twist)

Rhinestone

Chain Stitch

Back Stitch

Straight Stitch   French Knots (1 twist)

Back Stitch

Chain Stitch

French Knots
(2 twists)

Back Stitch

Back Stitch

Running Stitch

Rhinestone

Twisted Chain Stitch

Satin Stitch

Back Stitch

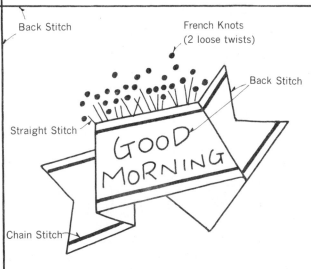

Back Stitch

French Knots
(2 loose twists)

Back Stitch

Straight Stitch

Chain Stitch

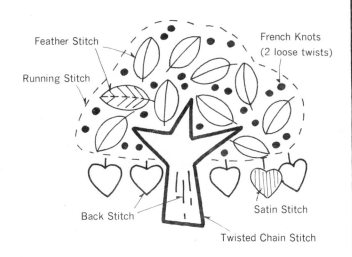

Feather Stitch

Running Stitch

French Knots
(2 loose twists)

Back Stitch

Satin Stitch

Twisted Chain Stitch

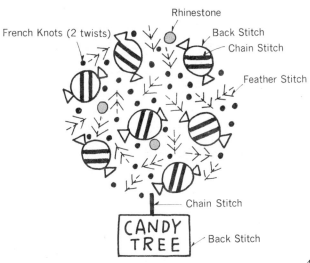

Rhinestone

French Knots (2 twists)

Back Stitch

Chain Stitch

Feather Stitch

Chain Stitch

CANDY
TREE

Back Stitch

T-shirt
Instructions on page 46.

T-shirt (P.44)

Materials:

Ready-to-wear T-shirt, 1 skein Blue-gray #25 embroidery floss.

Directions:

Embroider design on front of T-shirt.

Continued from P.6

Actual size

B

D

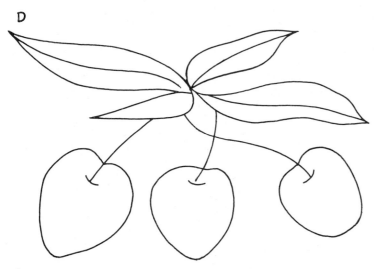

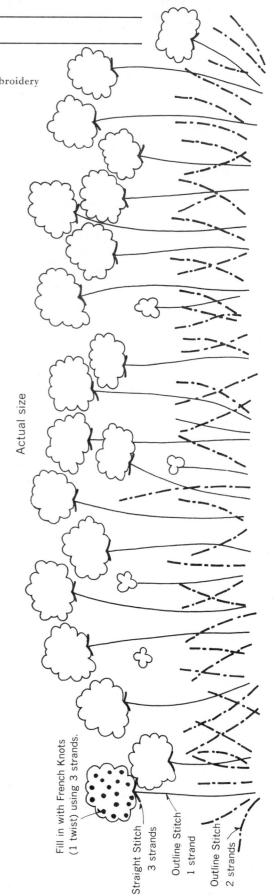

Actual size

Fill in with French Knots
(1 twist) using 3 strands.

Straight Stitch
3 strands

Outline Stitch
1 strand

Outline Stitch
2 strands

♯25 embroidery floss

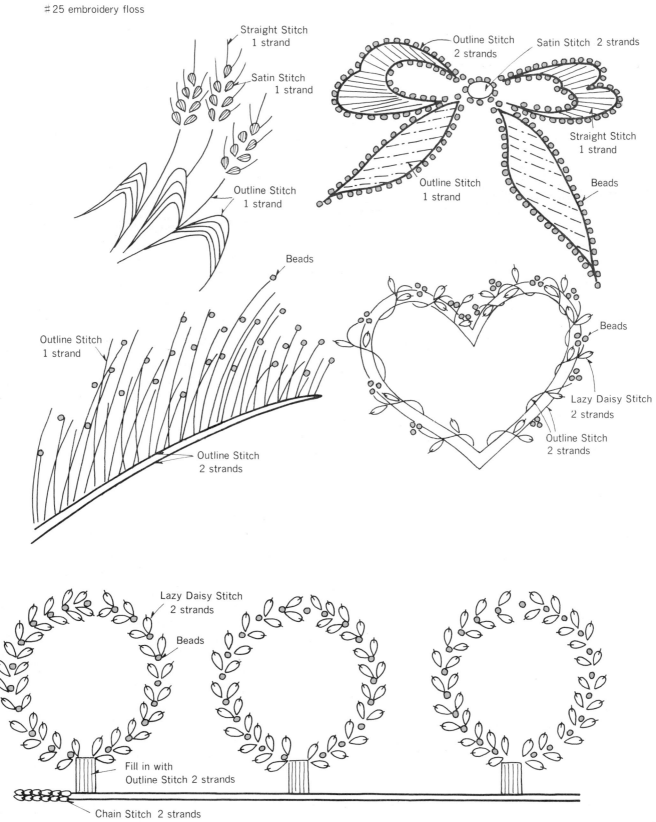

Straight Stitch
1 strand

Satin Stitch
1 strand

Outline Stitch
1 strand

Outline Stitch
2 strands

Satin Stitch 2 strands

Straight Stitch
1 strand

Outline Stitch
1 strand

Beads

Beads

Outline Stitch
1 strand

Outline Stitch
2 strands

Beads

Lazy Daisy Stitch
2 strands

Outline Stitch
2 strands

Lazy Daisy Stitch
2 strands

Beads

Fill in with
Outline Stitch 2 strands

Chain Stitch 2 strands

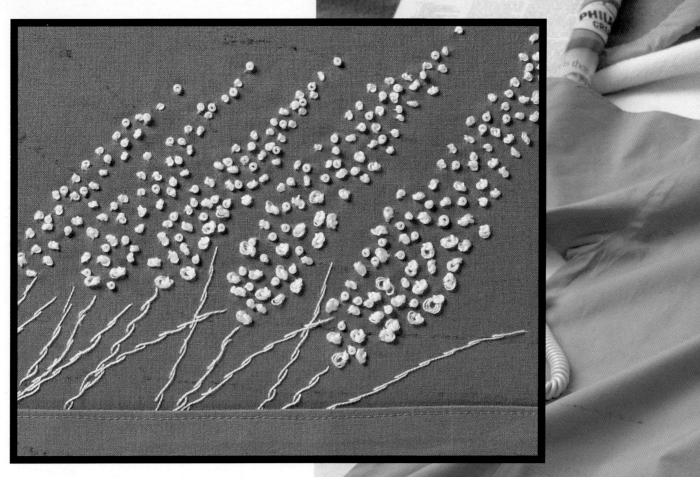

Relaxing at Home

Housecoat

Instructions on page 50.

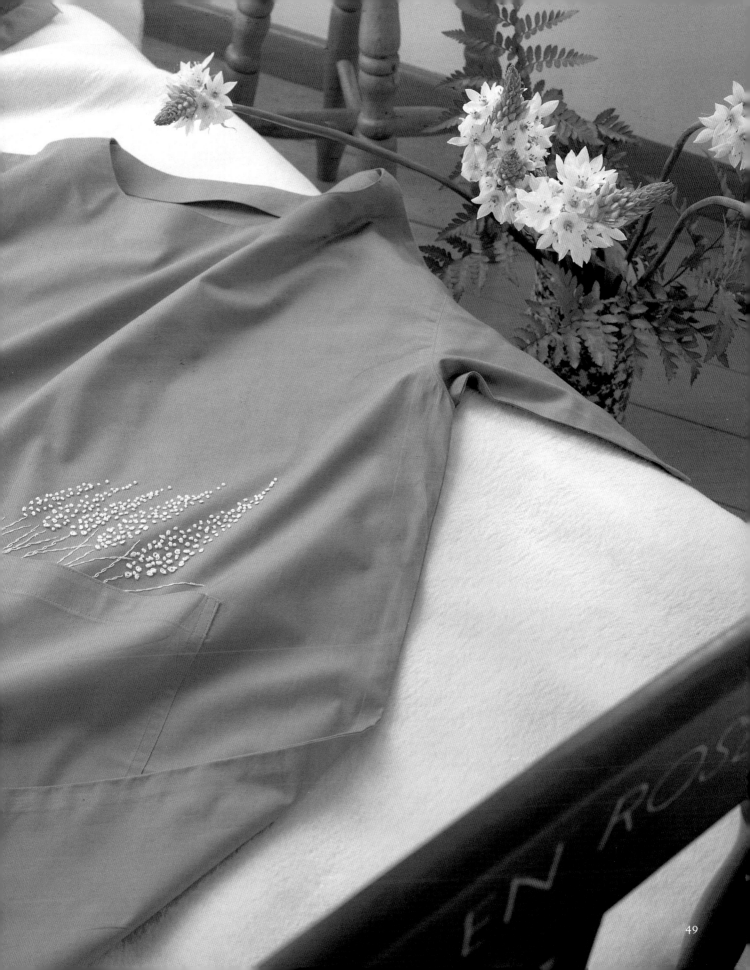

Materials:
Gray cotton 90cm×320cm (36"×128"),
Fusible interfacing 70cm×20cm (28"×8"),
102 Beads (small),
1 skein White #25 embroidery floss.
Finished size:
Refer to illustration.

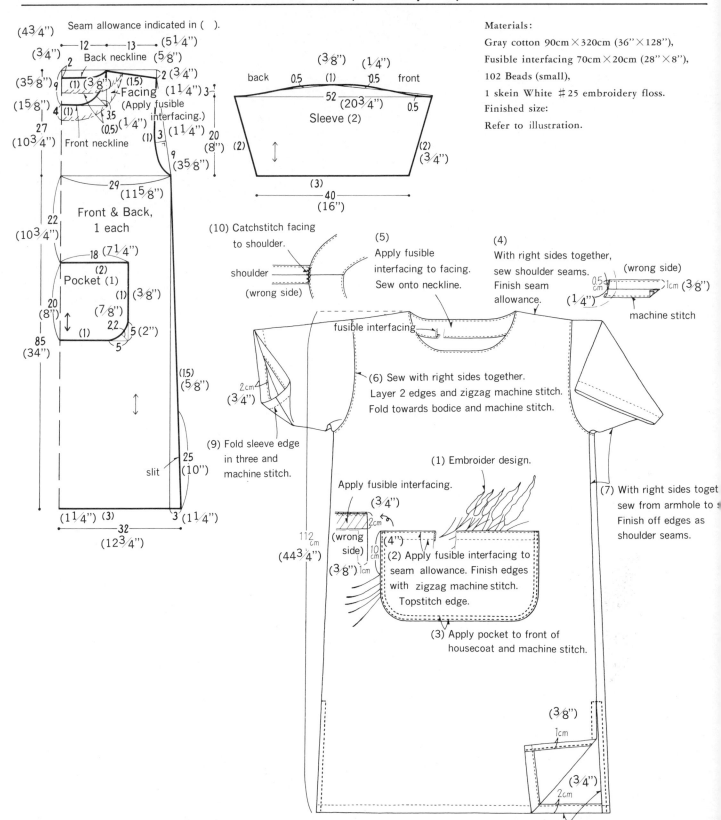

Seam allowance indicated in ( ).

(4¾")
12 — 13 (5¼")
(¾") 2 Back neckline (5⁄8")
(3⁄8") (1¼")
back 0.5 (1) 0.5 front
(3⁄8") 2 (¾")
(35⁄8") (1) (3⁄8") (1.5)
(15⁄8") 4 (1) Facing (1¼") 3
(Apply fusible
3.5 interfacing.)
(0.5) (¼")
27 Front neckline (1) 3 (1¼") 20
(103⁄4") 9 (8")
(35⁄8")
52 (203⁄4") 0.5
Sleeve (2)
(2) (2)
(¾")
29 (115⁄8")
22 Front & Back,
(103⁄4") 1 each
40
(16")

18 (7¼")
(2)
Pocket (1)
(1) (3⁄8")
20 (7⁄8")
(8") 2.2
(1) 5 (2")
5
85
(34")

slit

25
(10")

(1.5)
(5⁄8")

3 (1¼")
(1¼") (3)
32
(123⁄4")

(10) Catchstitch facing
to shoulder.
shoulder
(wrong side)

(5)
Apply fusible
interfacing to facing.
Sew onto neckline.

(4)
With right sides together,
sew shoulder seams.
Finish seam
allowance.

(wrong side)
0.5 cm 1cm (3⁄8")
(¼")
machine stitch

fusible interfacing

(6) Sew with right sides together.
Layer 2 edges and zigzag machine stitch.
Fold towards bodice and machine stitch.

2 cm
(¾")

(9) Fold sleeve edge
in three and
machine stitch.

(1) Embroider design.

(7) With right sides toget
sew from armhole to
Finish off edges as
shoulder seams.

Apply fusible interfacing.
(¾")
2cm
(wrong
side)
10 cm
(3⁄8") 1cm
(4")

112 cm
(44¾")

(2) Apply fusible interfacing to
seam allowance. Finish edges
with zigzag machine stitch.
Topstitch edge.

(3) Apply pocket to front of
housecoat and machine stitch.

(3⁄8")
1cm

(3⁄4")
2cm

(8) Fold hem in three and sew.
Then fold slit edge and machine stitch

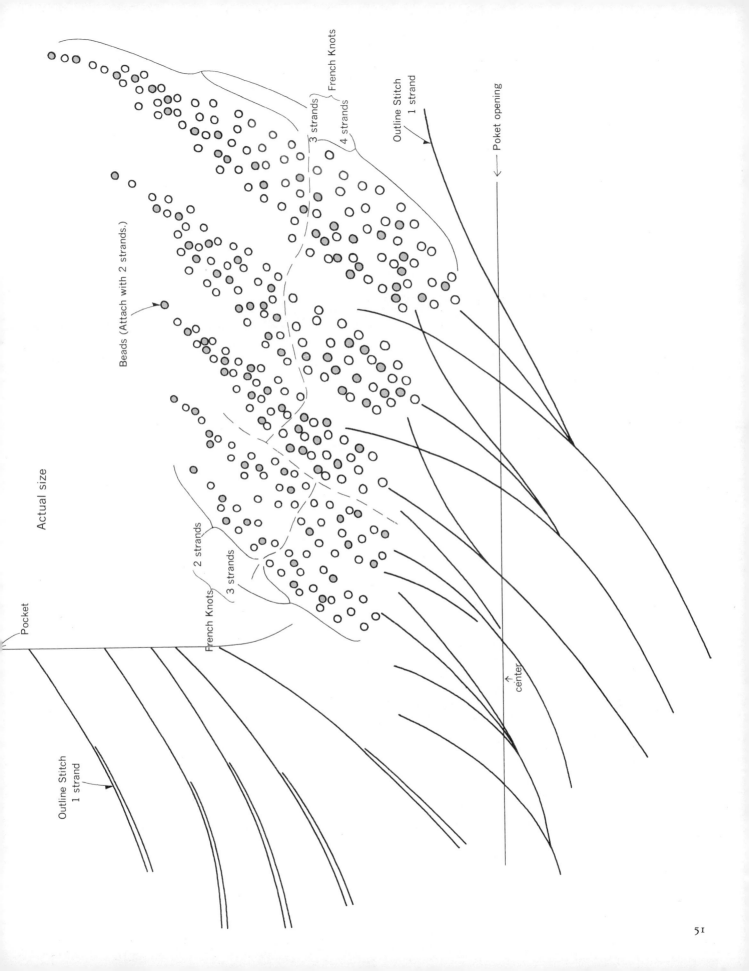

Actual size

Beads (Attach with 2 strands.)

French Knots
3 strands
4 strands

Outline Stitch
1 strand

Poket opening

center

Pocket

French Knots
2 strands
3 strands

Outline Stitch
1 strand

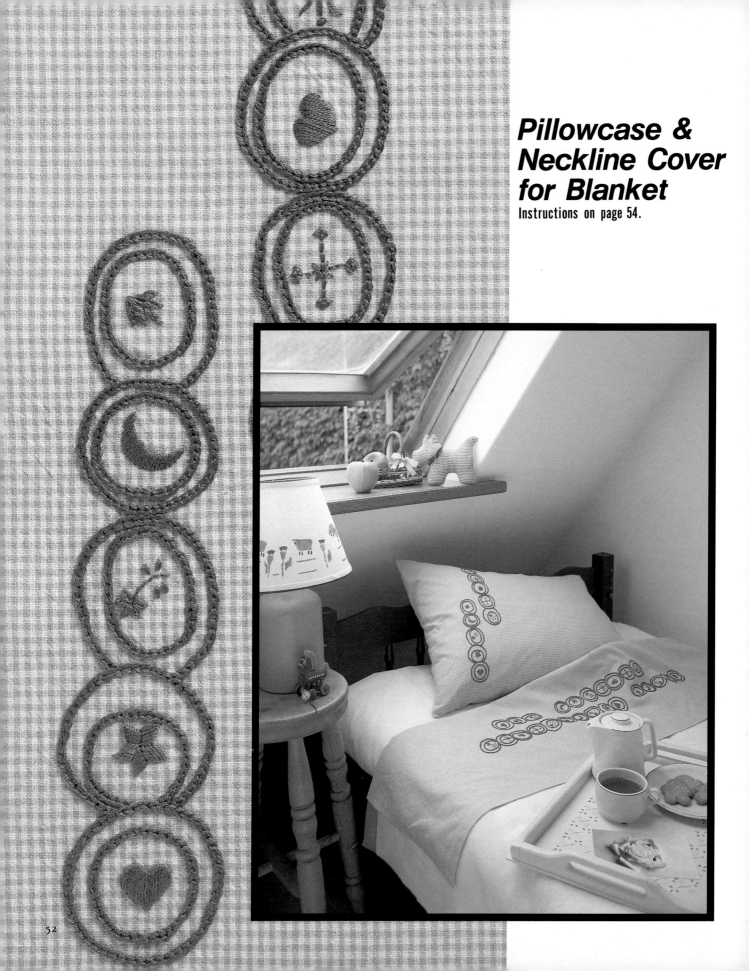

Pillowcase & Neckline Cover for Blanket

Instructions on page 54.

Pillowcase & Neckline Cover for Blanket (P.52)

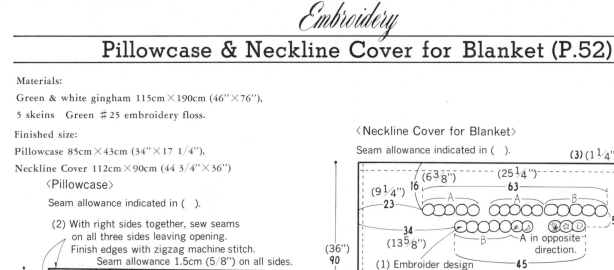

Materials:

Green & white gingham 115cm×190cm (46"×76"),

5 skeins   Green #25 embroidery floss.

Finished size:

Pillowcase 85cm×43cm (34"×17 1/4"),

Neckline Cover 112cm×90cm (44 3/4"×36")

〈Pillowcase〉

Seam allowance indicated in ( ).

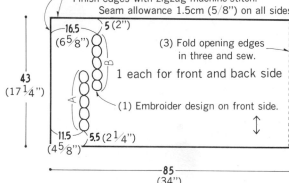

(2) With right sides together, sew seams
on all three sides leaving opening.
Finish edges with zigzag machine stitch.
Seam allowance 1.5cm (5/8") on all sides.

(3) Fold opening edges
in three and sew.

1 each for front and back side

(1) Embroider design on front side.

〈Neckline Cover for Blanket〉

Seam allowance indicated in ( ).

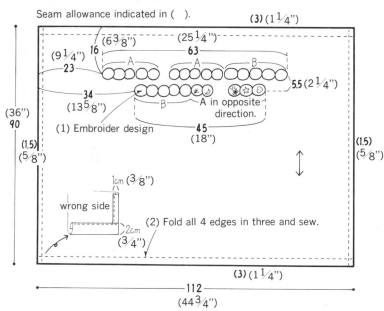

A in opposite direction.

(1) Embroider design

wrong side

(2) Fold all 4 edges in three and sew.

Use 3 strands unless indicated otherwise.

Actual size

A :

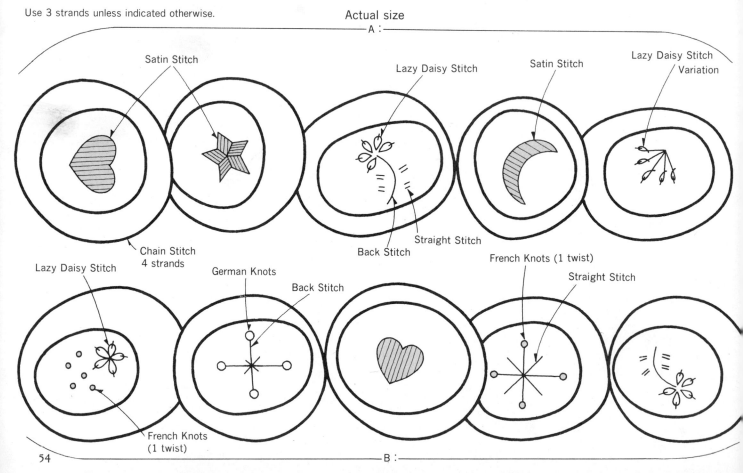

Satin Stitch

Lazy Daisy Stitch

Satin Stitch

Lazy Daisy Stitch Variation

Chain Stitch 4 strands

Back Stitch

Straight Stitch

French Knots (1 twist)

Lazy Daisy Stitch

German Knots

Back Stitch

Straight Stitch

French Knots (1 twist)

B :

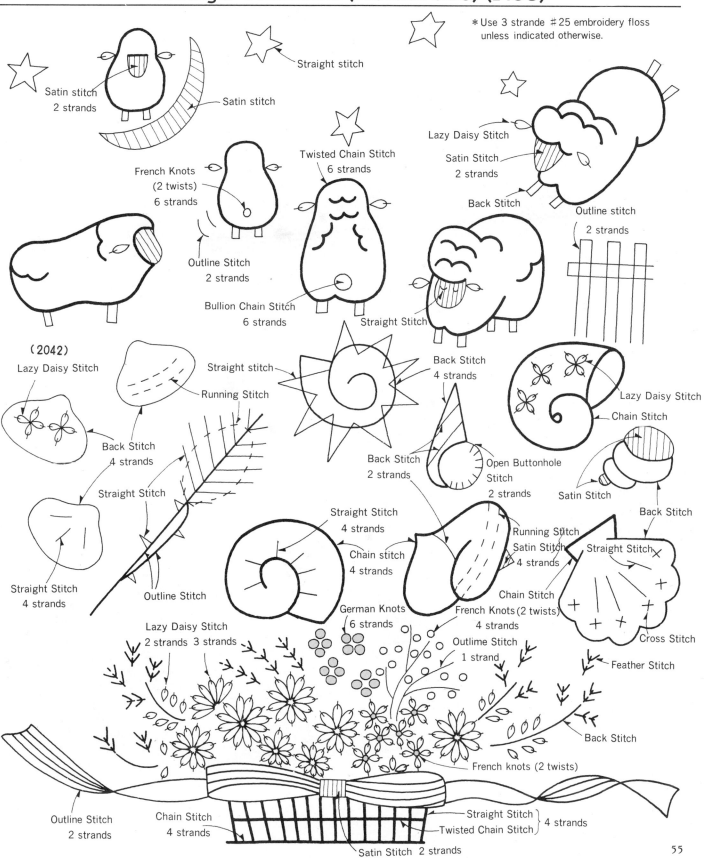

* Use 3 strande #25 embroidery floss unless indicated otherwise.

Satin stitch 2 strands

Straight stitch

Satin stitch

French Knots (2 twists) 6 strands

Twisted Chain Stitch 6 strands

Lazy Daisy Stitch

Satin Stitch 2 strands

Back Stitch

Outline stitch 2 strands

Outline Stitch 2 strands

Bullion Chain Stitch 6 strands

Straight Stitch

Back Stitch 4 strands

Lazy Daisy Stitch

Chain Stitch

(2042)

Lazy Daisy Stitch

Straight stitch

Running Stitch

Back Stitch 4 strands

Straight Stitch

Straight Stitch 4 strands

Outline Stitch

Back Stitch 2 strands

Open Buttonhole Stitch 2 strands

Satin Stitch

Back Stitch

Straight Stitch

Straight Stitch 4 strands

Chain stitch 4 strands

Running Stitch

Satin Stitch 4 strands

Chain Stitch

French Knots (2 twists) 4 strands

Cross Stitch

German Knots 6 strands

Outline Stitch 1 strand

Feather Stitch

Lazy Daisy Stitch 2 strands 3 strands

Back Stitch

French knots (2 twists)

Outline Stitch 2 strands

Chain Stitch 4 strands

Straight Stitch

Twisted Chain Stitch

4 strands

Satin Stitch 2 strands

Handy Bags

Drawstring Purse, Pouch & Small Drawstring Purse
Instructions on page 58.

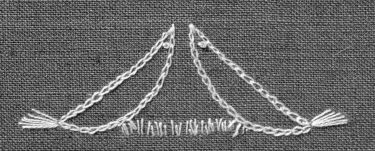

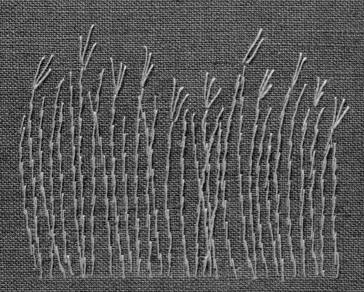

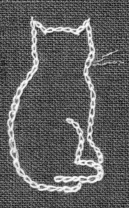

Drawstring Purse

Materials:

Blue pique fabric 54cm × 55cm (21 5/8" × 22"), 57 Beads (small), Cotton cord 0.5cm (1/4") diameter 140cm (56"), 0.5 skein Blue #25 embroidery floss.

Finished size:

Refer to illustration.

Seam allowance is 1cm (3/8").

Bag (1)

2.5 (1")   3 (1¼")   3 (1¼")

opening

20 (8")

(15⁄8") 4

←Place on fold.

25 (10")

Lid (2)

2.5 (1")

18 (7¼")   7 (2¾")

12.5 (5")

25 (10")

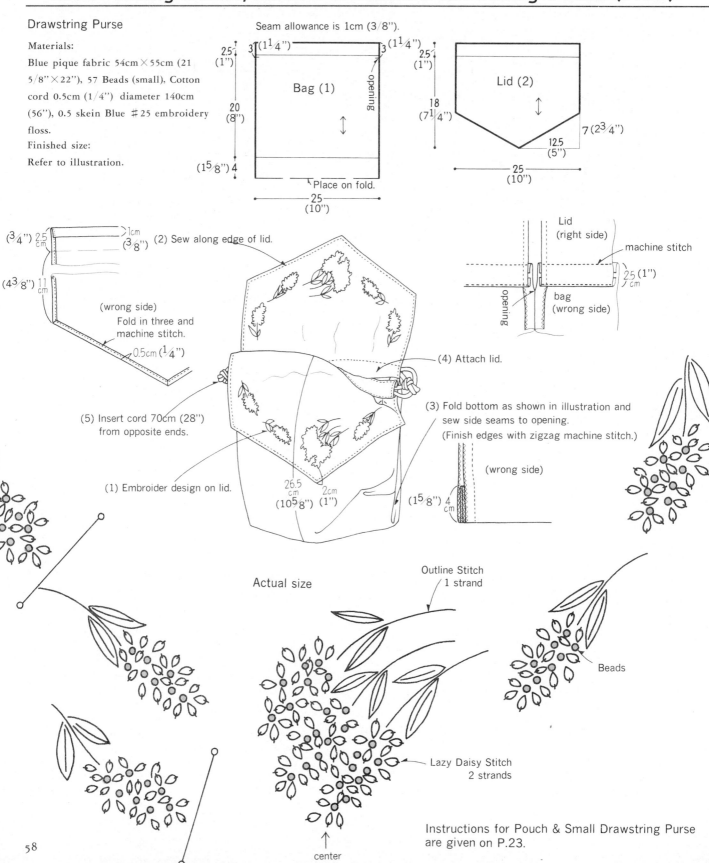

(2) Sew along edge of lid.

(3⁄4") 2.5 cm   1cm (3⁄8")

(43⁄8") 11 cm

(wrong side) Fold in three and machine stitch.

0.5cm (1⁄4")

Lid (right side)   machine stitch

2.5 (1") cm

opening   bag (wrong side)

(4) Attach lid.

(5) Insert cord 70cm (28") from opposite ends.

(3) Fold bottom as shown in illustration and sew side seams to opening. (Finish edges with zigzag machine stitch.)

(wrong side)

(15⁄8") 4 cm

(1) Embroider design on lid.

26.5 cm (105⁄8")   2cm (1")

Actual size

Outline Stitch 1 strand

Beads

Lazy Daisy Stitch 2 strands

center

Instructions for Pouch & Small Drawstring Purse are given on P.23.

Use 1 strand #25 embroidery floss unless indicated otherwise.

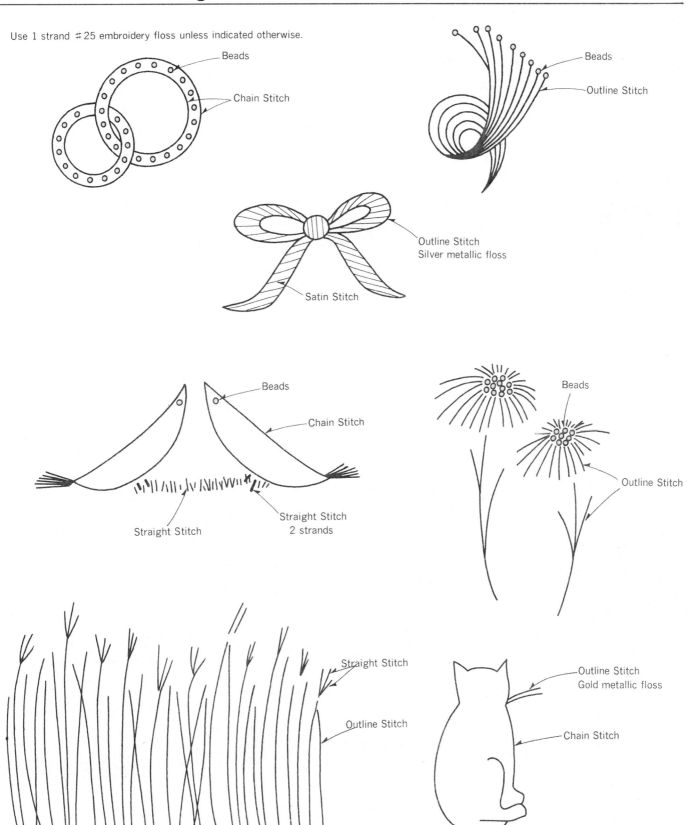

Beads

Chain Stitch

Beads

Outline Stitch

Outline Stitch
Silver metallic floss

Satin Stitch

Beads

Chain Stitch

Straight Stitch

Straight Stitch
2 strands

Beads

Outline Stitch

Straight Stitch

Outline Stitch

Outline Stitch
Gold metallic floss

Chain Stitch

Memorable Times

Clock

Instructions on page 62.

Clock

Instructions on page 62.

Materials:

(P.60)

Printed cotton fabric 23cm×23cm (9 1/4") square, White & black ♯25 embroidery floss, White frame (for clay work) : outside dimension 20cm×20cm (8"×8") square, inside dimension 16.5cm ×16.5cm (6 5/8"×6 5/8"), Cardboard 16.3cm×16.3cm (6 1/2"× 6 1/2") square.

(P.61)

Beige twilled linen 21cm×21cm (8 3/8"×8 3/8"), Charcoal-gray & Black ♯25 embroidery floss,

Round Frame (for mosaic work) :
   outside dimension 21cm (8 3/8") diameter,
   inside dimension 15cm (6") diamerter,
Cardboard 14.8cm (5 7/8") diameter,
Brown paint.

Actual size

Use 2 strands and Back Stitch unless indicated otherwise.

(P.64)

Light brown linen 25cm×25cm (10"×10") square,

Gray-brown, black ♯25 embroidery floss,

Hexagon frame (for mosaic work) :
   outside dimension 25.5cm×22cm (10 1/4"×8 3/4"),
   inside dimension 18.5cm×16cm (7 3/8"×6 3/8"),
Cardoard 18.3cm×15.8cm (7 3/8"×6 3/8").

(For all clocks, you will need the following :)
   Handmade clock movement : Craftclock Slim Quartz (S-2000),
   white hands (DQ-11W).

Directions :

Embroider design. Add 3cm (1 1/4") seam allowance to inside dimension of frame and cut embroidered piece in that size. Glue to cardboard and fit into frame. Assemble clock. Paint frame for clock on P.61.

(P.64)

Feather Stitch and Straight Stitch 2 strands

Straight Stitch 1 strand

center

Feather Stitch 1 strand

Outline Stitch 2 strands

Back Stitch 1 strand

Feather Stitch and Straight Stitch 2 strands

Straight Stitch 1 strand

Straight Stitch 1 strand

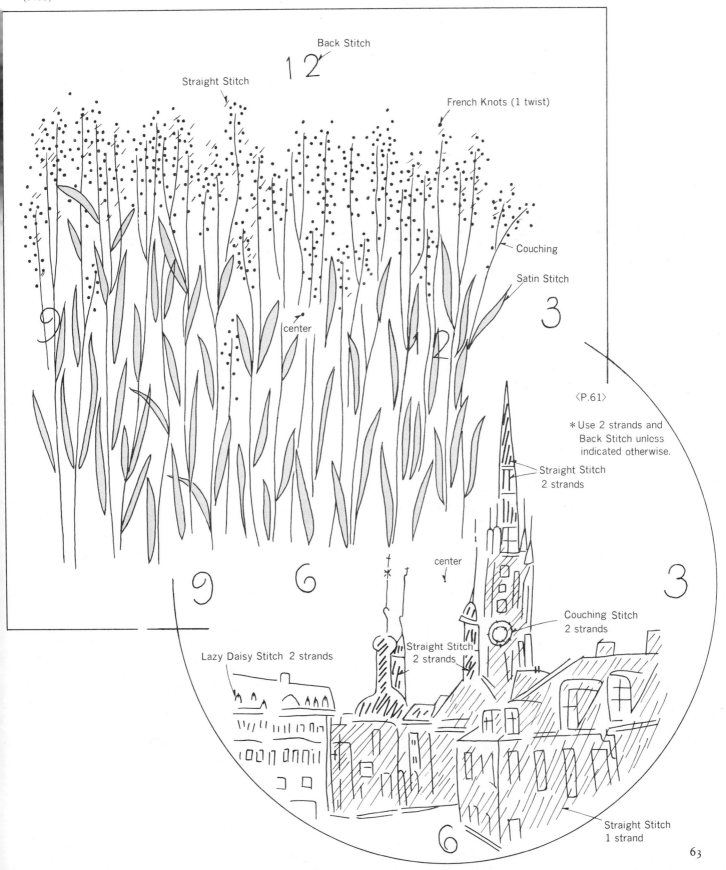

Actual size   Ues 2 strands unless indicated otherwise.

Back Stitch

12

Straight Stitch

French Knots (1 twist)

Couching

Satin Stitch

3

center

〈P.61〉

*Use 2 strands and
Back Stitch unless
indicated otherwise.

Straight Stitch
2 strands

center

3

9

6

Couching Stitch
2 strands

Lazy Daisy Stitch 2 strands

Straight Stitch
2 strands

Straight Stitch
1 strand

6

Clock
Instructions on page 62.